HOW TO SAVE TIME AND TANGLES
Copyright © 2022 by KRISTALIZED INC.
ISBN: 979-8-9869100-5-5
Library of Congress Control Number is on file.
Published in Austin, Texas
All rights reserved. No part of this publication may be reproduced, distributed, or transmitted in any form or by any means, including photocopying, recording, or other electronic or mechanical methods, without the prior written permission of the publisher or author, except in the case of brief quotations embodied in critical reviews and certain other noncommercial uses permitted by copyright law.
Although every precaution has been taken to verify the accuracy of the information contained herein, the author and publisher assume no responsibility for any errors or omissions. No liability is assumed for damages that may result from the use of information contained within.

Thank you Kristany Jackson for your photography contributions in the book.
Love you dearly!

# Kristalized Kuties Book Series

## How to Save Time and Tangles

**KRISTALIZED INC.**

# Hi, I'm Kristal!

Thank you for picking up this book on how to save time and tangles. You will learn how to properly shampoo, condition, detangle, and blow-dry your hair. You will also learn product placement. So, let's get started!

First, we put the hair into four sections, this is how you save tangles! Use 4 clips to keep each section in place.

Next, grab a spray bottle and wet one section of your hair. Using a small amount of shampoo, work it through one section at a time so that you have more control without tangling your hair.

......................................

Using a shampoo brush, start brushing the ends, slowly working your way to your scalp. The shampoo brush stimulates blood flow to your follicles.

You want to pay EXTRA close attention to your scalp to ensure it is clean. Think of your scalp as the soil of your garden. You have to nurture and take care of it for your hair to grow strong. Clip that section as shown, move to the next, and repeat.

Now it's time to rinse. This part is best done in the shower. Rinse each section separately and clip when done. It's very important to rinse in a downward motion. DO NOT FLIP YOUR HEAD OVER/UPSIDE DOWN – This causes tangles.

Rinse in the direction your hair grows. Hold your head back while running your fingers through your hair to help the shampoo rinse out. Move to the next section and repeat. Don't forget to clip each section when you are done.

Now it's time to apply the conditioner to each section as you did with the shampoo. Instead of using the shampoo brush, you will now use the shower comb. Apply the conditioner to one section at a time starting at your ends and working your way to the scalp. Gently comb the conditioner in each section, twist, and re-clip. Move to the next section and repeat.

The conditioner needs to stay in your hair for 3 to 5 minutes (that's equivalent to listening to 2 of your favorite songs). Unclip one section at a time and rinse the conditioner out thoroughly, wring the water out, twist, clip, and repeat.

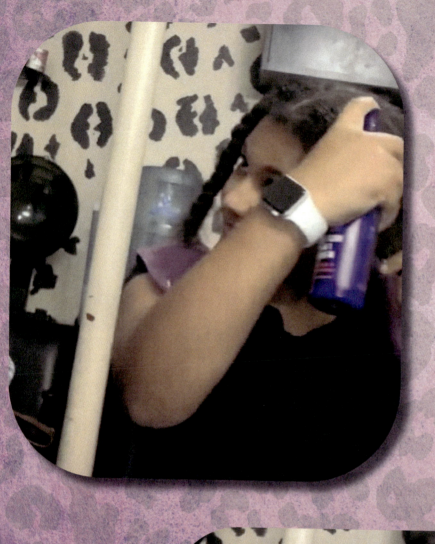

It's time to detangle! Spray leave-in conditioner and a small amount of moisturizer on one section. Using a wide-tooth comb, start combing at the ends, and work your way to the roots. You're going to braid this section when you are done combing it out. Using this technique will save time and prepare your hair for blow-drying.

......................................

Your natural hair can air dry as long as it is detangled first and then twisted OR braided while wet. Natural hair shrinks so it tangles and it's much easier to comb when wet than dry. Braiding it will keep it stretched and detangled until you are ready to blow dry or style.

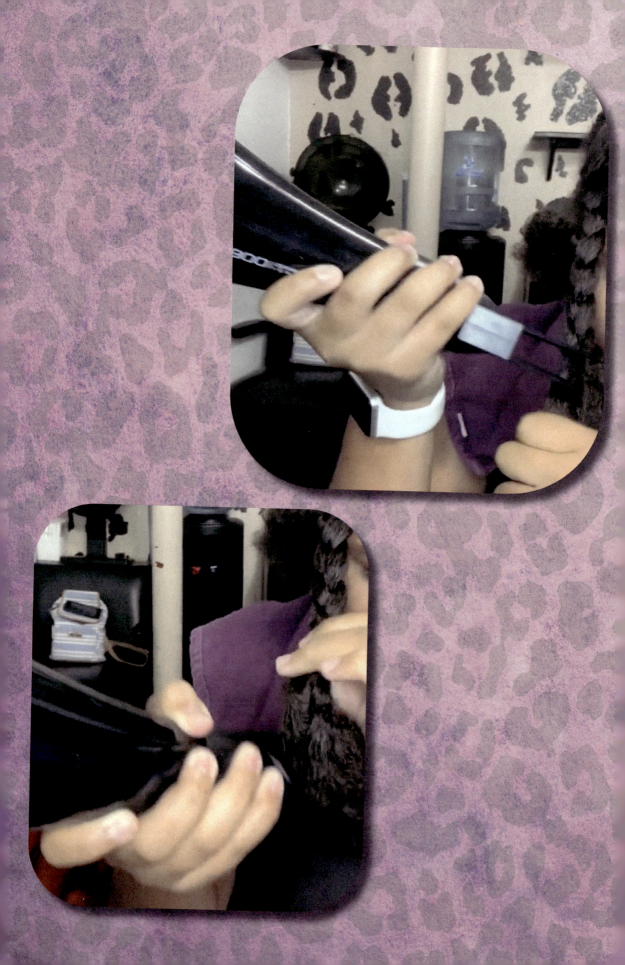

Blow-dryer time! Do not unbraid your hair yet. Instead, put the comb of the blow dryer into the end of the braid and SLOWLY comb out the braid. This technique is important! The focus here is to move slowly, making sure the warm air gets to every strand of hair. Use patience and let the blow dryer do its job. Tools are used to make things easier. Work your way up to your scalp, clip, and repeat in the remaining sections.

Now that your hair is completely blow-dried you may prep it to style. Twist or braid it as the last step. You can use edge control on your edges while using a vent brush to neatly put your hair into a ponytail. You can also do twists or braids without ponytails. Make the twists medium or large and use a roller on the ends to keep them in place. Use a silk hair wrap to secure your edges.

Now that you have the skills and tools, be a confident
**KRISTALIZED KUTIE!**

# Affirmations:

☆ I am learning to take care of my hair.
☆ I love myself and I love my hair.
☆ My hair is strong and healthy.
☆ I will take care of my scalp.
☆ I define my beauty, no one else.
☆ My hair enhances my beauty.
☆ My hair is naturally beautiful.
☆ I have the skills to take care of my hair.
☆ Taking care of my hair is self-care.
☆ My hair looks great on me.
☆ Taking care of my hair is easy.
☆ My hair looks great in any hairstyle I choose.
☆ My curl pattern is gorgeous.
☆ My curl pattern is easy to manage.
☆ I deserve healthy hair.
☆ I will be patient with my hair.
☆ My hair makes me feel confident.

Pick your 5 favorite affirmations and make sure to say them to yourself out loud every day.

Practice this routine and share it with friends and family. Take care of your hair and love yourself. ♡

Special thanks to:

☆ My husband Otis
☆ My daughter Kristany
☆ My sons Kason and Kobe
☆ Granddaughter Gloria
☆ In loving memory of my mother Stephanie Ann

# Thank you to all the
# Kristalized Kuties!

# Meet the Author:

**Kristal** was born and raised in Arlington, TX. From a very young age, she developed a natural talent for hair and beauty. Inspired by her own personal hair journey, she aspired to become "Thee Kristalizer" and has been proudly serving adults and Kristalized Kuties across the Dallas/Fort Worth area with excellent service for the past 20 years. In addition to on-time appointments and quality service, Kristal focuses on hair health and style longevity by providing maintenance, tips and tricks, as well as offering an array of Kristalized products, merchandise, and tools available for purchase. Determined to extend her knowledge to Kristalized Kuties everywhere, she has written *How to Save Time and Tangles* and she hopes will help teach all Kuties across the world how to care for and love their hair while saving time and tangles. In addition to hair, she's most proud of her humanitarian efforts to the homeless community through her Christmas sock drive in honor of her mother who passed away in 2014. She was also a hairstylist and continues to be a driving force in Kristal's connection from hair to heart. Kristal also serves her community by volunteering at local career days.

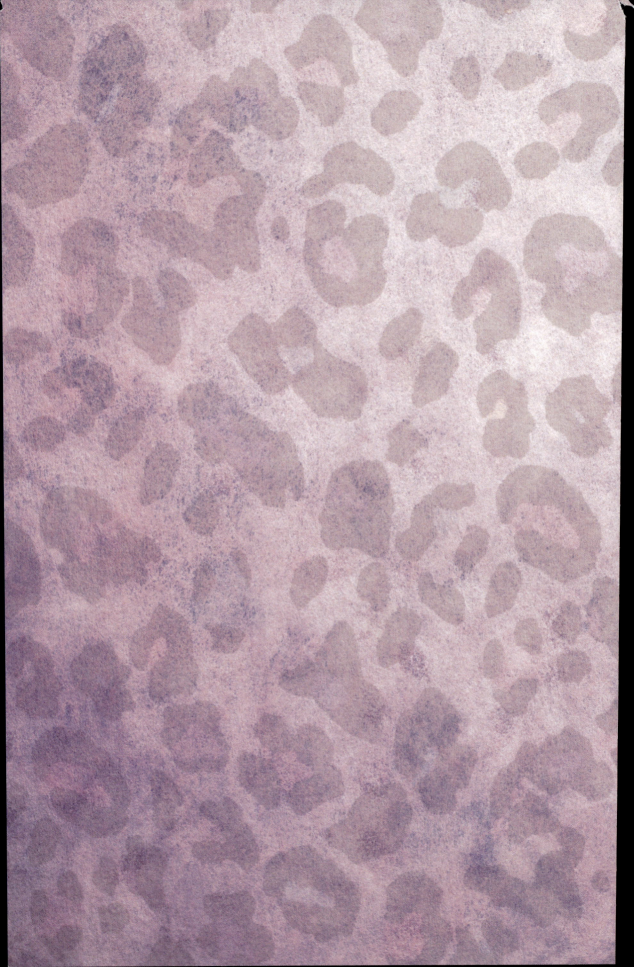

# *Kristalized*

crys·tal·lized | /ˈkristəˌlīzd/

*adjective*

1: to have your hair revitalized by "Thee Kristalizer"

2: to cause to take a definite form

3: made clear or definite

105 Publishing LLC
Austin, TX
www.105publishing.com

Made in the USA
Middletown, DE
15 October 2022